D0915060

PRESIDENTS

WARREN G. HARDING

A MyReportLinks.com Book

Randy Schultz

 MyReportLinks.com Books
an imprint of
Enslow Publishers, Inc.
Box 398, 40 Industrial Road
Berkeley Heights, NJ 07922
USA

MyReportLinks.com Books, an imprint of Enslow Publishers, Inc. MyReportLinks is a trademark of Enslow Publishers, Inc.

Library of Congress Cataloging-in-Publication Data

Schultz, Randy.
  Warren G. Harding / Randy Schultz.
      p. cm. — (Presidents)
Summary: A biography of the twenty-ninth president of the United States, whose administration was best known for the Teapot Dome Scandal. Includes Internet links to Web sites, source documents, and photographs related to Warren G. Harding.
Includes bibliographical references and index.
  ISBN 0-7660-5103-X
1. Harding, Warren G. (Warren Gamaliel), 1865–1923—Juvenile literature. 2. Presidents—United States—Biography—Juvenile literature. [1. Harding, Warren G. (Warren Gamaliel), 1865–1923. 2. Presidents.] I. Title. II. Series.
E786 .S38 2003
973.91'4'092—dc21

                    2002014703

Printed in the United States of America

10 9 8 7 6 5 4 3 2 1

To Our Readers:
Through the purchase of this book, you and your library gain access to the Report Links that specifically back up this book.

The Publisher will provide access to the Report Links that back up this book and will keep these Report Links up to date on **www.myreportlinks.com** for three years from the book's first publication date.

We have done our best to make sure all Internet addresses in this book were active and appropriate when we went to press. However, the author and the Publisher have no control over, and assume no liability for, the material available on those Internet sites or on other Web sites they may link to.

The usage of the MyReportLinks.com Books Web site is subject to the terms and conditions stated on the Usage Policy Statement on **www.myreportlinks.com**.

A password may be required to access the Report Links that back up this book. The password is found on the bottom of page 4 of this book.

Any comments or suggestions can be sent by e-mail to comments@myreportlinks.com or to the address on the back cover.

Contents

MyReportLinks.com Books
Great Books, Great Links, Great for Research!

MyReportLinks.com Books present the information you need to learn about your report subject. In addition, they show you where to go on the Internet for more information. The pre-evaluated Report Links that back up this book are kept up to date on **www.myreportlinks.com**. With the purchase of a MyReportLinks.com Books title, you and your library gain access to the Report Links that specifically back up that book. The Report Links save hours of research time and link to dozens—even hundreds—of Web sites, source documents, and photos related to your report topic.

Please see "To Our Readers" on the Copyright page for important information about this book, the MyReportLinks.com Books Web site, and the Report Links that back up this book.

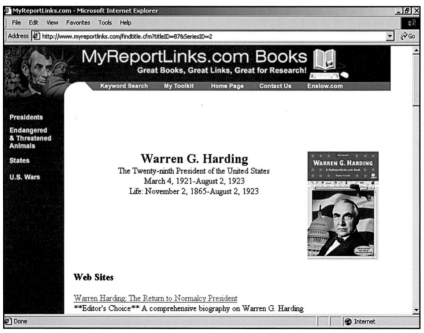

Access:

The Publisher will provide access to the Report Links that back up this book and will try to keep these Report Links up to date on our Web site for three years from the book's first publication date. Please enter **PHA5655** if asked for a password.

Report Links

 The Internet sites described below can be accessed at
http://www.myreportlinks.com

*EDITOR'S CHOICE

▶ **Warren Harding: The Return to Normalcy President**
This comprehensive biography about Warren G. Harding discusses
his early life, presidential campaigns, domestic and foreign affairs,
the First Lady, and his legacy. You will also find images, quotes, and
additional resources.

Link to this Internet site from http://www.myreportlinks.com

*EDITOR'S CHOICE

▶ **American Presidents: Life Portraits—Warren G. Harding**
The American Presidents Life Portraits Web site provides quick facts
and figures about Warren G. Harding. You will also find an image
gallery, his inaugural address, and a letter from Harding to an
ambassador in which he discusses golf.

Link to this Internet site from http://www.myreportlinks.com

*EDITOR'S CHOICE

▶ **Objects from the Presidency**
By navigating through this site you will find objects related to all the
American presidents, including Warren G. Harding. You can also read
a brief description of Harding and the era he lived in and learn about
the office of the presidency.

Link to this Internet site from http://www.myreportlinks.com

*EDITOR'S CHOICE

▶ **Presidents of the United States:
Warren Gamaliel Harding**
The POTUS Web site provides facts and figures on Warren G. Harding.
Here you will find election results, cabinet appointments, information
about Harding's family, and important events in his administration.

Link to this Internet site from http://www.myreportlinks.com

*EDITOR'S CHOICE

▶ **"I Do Solemnly Swear . . . "**
Experience Warren G. Harding's inauguration through images and
documents. Here you will find a telegram and a letter from Harding to
the inauguration committee, a link to his inaugural address, and other
pieces of memorabilia.

Link to this Internet site from http://www.myreportlinks.com

*EDITOR'S CHOICE

▶ **Warren Gamaliel Harding, 29th President**
The *New York Times* Learning Network's Web site contains a page of
Harding facts. Some of the topics included are Harding's mysterious
death, the Teapot Dome scandal, and journalist H. L. Mencken's
criticism of the president's choice of words.

Link to this Internet site from http://www.myreportlinks.com

Report Links

 The Internet sites described below can be accessed at
http://www.myreportlinks.com

The American Presidency: Teapot Dome
The American Presidency Web site offers a concise overview of the origins of
the Teapot Dome scandal, its resulting trials, and its legacy.

Link to this Internet site from http://www.myreportlinks.com

The American Presidency: Warren Harding
The American Presidency Web site offers a biography of Warren G. Harding.
His inaugural address and a quick reference guide can also be found here.

Link to this Internet site from http://www.myreportlinks.com

The American President: Calvin Coolidge: The Passive President
This comprehensive Web site provides detailed information about Warren G.
Harding's vice president and successor, Calvin Coolidge. Here you will learn
about his life and work before, during, and after his presidency.

Link to this Internet site from http://www.myreportlinks.com

The American Presidential Election: Washington Conference
The International Conference on Naval Limitation, otherwise known as the
Washington Naval Conference, met to limit the naval arms race and discuss
problems in East Asia. This Web site provides an overview of the conference.

Link to this Internet site from http://www.myreportlinks.com

Clash of Cultures in the 1910s and 1920s
The conflict between Victorian and modern morals characterized life in the
1920s. This site from the Ohio State Department of History focuses on
prohibition, immigration restrictions, the Ku Klux Klan, the new woman,
and the Scopes trial.

Link to this Internet site from http://www.myreportlinks.com

DCBA Brief Online: Harding and the Scandals
This page examines the Veterans Bureau, Teapot Dome, and other scandals
that were part of Warren G. Harding's administration.

Link to this Internet site from http://www.myreportlinks.com

Report Links

➤ The Internet sites described below can be accessed at
http://www.myreportlinks.com

▶ Factmonster: Harding, Warren Gamaliel

Factmonster provides a brief introduction to Warren G. Harding.
Some topics covered are the Teapot Dome scandal and the Washington
Naval Conference.

Link to this Internet site from http://www.myreportlinks.com

▶ Friends of Harding Home and Memorial

The Friends of Harding Home and Memorial is dedicated to the
preservation and promotion of the Harding Home, the house from
which Warren G. Harding conducted his front porch presidential
campaign in 1920.

Link to this Internet site from http://www.myreportlinks.com

▶ The Harding Story

Warren Harding, an advocate of homeopathic medicine, ignored the
medical innovations of his day. Here you will learn how the president's
life may have been saved had he received the proper care.

Link to this Internet site from http://www.myreportlinks.com

▶ The History of the League of Nations

The United Nations Office in Geneva's Web site holds a history of
the League of Nations. You will also find a library that has related
documents, biographies, essays, and bibliographic information; a
gallery with images of events, portraits, posters and cartoons; and more.

Link to this Internet site from http://www.myreportlinks.com

▶ The *Marion Star*

When Warren G. Harding was young, he and two friends bought the
Marion Star, a local newspaper in Ohio. At this Web site you can read
the newspaper.

Link to this Internet site from http://www.myreportlinks.com

▶ NARA: Exhibit Hall: The Constitution: The 19th Amendment

The National Archives and Records Administration's Web site holds
this article about the 1920 passage of the Nineteenth Amendment,
granting women the right to vote.

Link to this Internet site from http://www.myreportlinks.com

Report Links

The Internet sites described below can be accessed at
http://www.myreportlinks.com

One Lesson From History: Appointment of Special Council and the Investigation of the Teapot Dome Scandal
This Web site contains a comprehensive report about the Teapot Dome investigation. Provided are government documents, congressional records, court transcripts, and newspaper articles related to the scandal.

Link to this Internet site from http://www.myreportlinks.com

President Warren Gamaliel Harding
Thinkquest's profile of Warren G. Harding reviews the highlights of his years in office. Here you will find an interesting fact about Harding, a quote, a list of important events of his presidency, a list of his cabinet members, and a brief biography.

Link to this Internet site from http://www.myreportlinks.com

The Presidential Election of 1920
American Memory, a Library of Congress Web site, contains a page about the 1920 presidential election. Audio files of speeches by Warren Harding, Calvin Coolidge, Corinne Roosevelt Robinson, James Cox, and Franklin D. Roosevelt can be found here.

Link to this Internet site from http://www.myreportlinks.com

Prohibition: A Case Study in Progressive Reform
The Eighteenth Amendment to the Constitution prohibited the manufacture, transportation, and sale of alcoholic beverages. This site from the Library of Congress Learning Page tells the story of Prohibition through the accounts of people who lived through it.

Link to this Internet site from http://www.myreportlinks.com

United States Senate: November 2, 1920: A Senator Becomes President
The United States Senate Series of Historical Minutes Web site contains an article about how Warren G. Harding and John F. Kennedy were the only two incumbent senators in U.S. history to win the presidential election.

Link to this Internet site from http://www.myreportlinks.com

The Versailles Treaty
In addition to the complete text of the Versailles Treaty, this site includes maps, photos, cartoons, and chronologies of World War I and Wilson's subsequent battle with Congress for approval of the League of Nations.

Link to this Internet site from http://www.myreportlinks.com

Report Links

 The Internet sites described below can be accessed at
http://www.myreportlinks.com

▶ **Warren G. Harding calls for a "Return to Normalcy,"
Boston, MA, May 14, 1920.**
Here you will find the text of Warren Harding's famous "Return to
Normalcy" speech, in which Harding summed up the national desire
for calm after the turbulent events of World War I.

Link to this Internet site from http://www.myreportlinks.com

▶ **Warren G. Harding's Inaugural Address**
Bartleby.com holds the inaugural address of Warren G. Harding.
Harding was the first sitting senator to be elected president. In his
address, Harding speaks about World War I, women's suffrage,
taxation, tariffs, and other important issues of the time.

Link to this Internet site from http://www.myreportlinks.com

▶ **Warren Harding's Obituary**
This Web site holds Harding's obituary from the *New York Times*.
The obituary discusses President Warren G. Harding's final days and
the courage of First Lady Florence Harding.

Link to this Internet site from http://www.myreportlinks.com

▶ **The White House: Florence Kling Harding**
The official White House Web site holds the biography of First Lady
Florence Kling Harding. Here you will learn about her early life, her
marriage to Harding, and her years as First Lady.

Link to this Internet site from http://www.myreportlinks.com

▶ **The White House: Warren G. Harding**
The official White House Web site holds the biography of
Warren G. Harding. Here you will learn about Harding's life,
election, and presidency.

Link to this Internet site from http://www.myreportlinks.com

▶ *World Almanac for Kids Online:* **Warren G. Harding**
At the *World Almanac for Kids Online* Web site you will find a brief
profile of Warren G. Harding. Here you will learn about his presidency,
domestic and foreign policies, and his later years.

Link to this Internet site from http://www.myreportlinks.com

Highlights

1865—*Nov. 2:* Warren G. Harding is born on a farm near Corsica (present-day Blooming Grove), Ohio.

1880—Enrolls in Ohio Central College.

1882—Graduates from Ohio Central College.

1891—*July 8:* Marries Florence "Flossie" Mabel Kling DeWolfe.

1899—Elected to Ohio state senate.

1903—Elected lieutenant governor of Ohio.

1914—World War I breaks out in Europe.

—Elected to the United States Senate.

1920—Elected twenty-ninth president of the United States.

1921—*March 4:* Inauguration Day. Harding is the first president to ride to his inauguration in an automobile.

—*Nov. 11:* Dedicates the Tomb of the Unknown Soldier at Arlington National Cemetery.

1922—Committees of the U.S. Senate and a special commission begin investigating what becomes known as the Teapot Dome scandal.

—*March 29:* Five countries sign the Limitation on Naval Arms Treaty.

—*June 14:* Is the first president to broadcast a speech over the radio.

1923—*June 20:* Sets out on a "voyage of understanding."

—*July 8:* Becomes first president to visit Alaska.

—*July 26:* Becomes first president to visit Canada.

—*Aug. 2:* Dies in San Francisco, California.

Inauguration, 1921

At the stroke of one o'clock, on the afternoon of March 4, 1921, Warren Gamaliel Harding was sworn in as the twenty-ninth president of the United States. It was a moment that Harding himself could not believe was happening, since only months earlier, many felt he was not even a serious candidate for the highest office in the United States.

Americans wanted a change. They were tired of war-time restraints and world problems. The voters wanted someone stable and easygoing that would return the mood

▲ En route to his inauguration, Warren G. Harding is seated in the back seat of a convertible to the right of outgoing president Woodrow Wilson. Two once-prominent Republican leaders—Philander Knox, a former attorney general, and Joseph Cannon, formerly Speaker of the House—are seated in front.

of the country to the more carefree atmosphere of pre-World War I days.

These citizens opposed the policies of President Woodrow Wilson, including Wilson's definition of American ideals, and his unwillingness to accept any changes in his plan for a League of Nations. The League was an early version of the United Nations. Many Americans opposed joining the League because they thought it would pull America into unnecessary wars.

People just wanted to resume their normal lives with as little bother as possible coming from any place else in the world. That is all they were asking of Harding, and he felt that his administration could fulfill that wish.

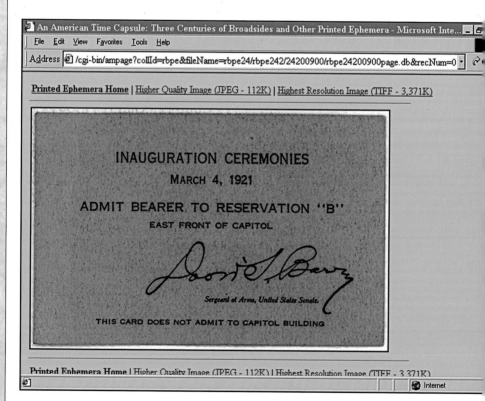

An invitation to President Harding's inauguration on March 4, 1921.

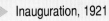

American Memory Digital Item Display - 00650966 - Microsoft Internet Explorer

e   Edit   View   Favorites   Tools   Help   Links »

dress   ?ammem/pin:@field(NUMBER+@band(ppmsc+02902)):displayType=1:m856sd=ppmsc:m856sf=02902   Go

Done   Internet

▲ *President Warren G. Harding, on the steps of the U.S. Capitol, waving to the crowd at his inauguration, March 4, 1921.*

In his inaugural address to the nation, Harding seized upon the country's mood, offering words of comfort.

> Our supreme task is the resumption of our onward normal way. Reconstruction, readjustment, restoration—all these must follow.

> If it will lighten the spirit and add to the resolution with which we take up the task, let me repeat for our Nation, we shall give no people just cause to make war upon us . . . If, despite this attitude, war is again forced upon us, I earnestly hope a way may be found which will unify our individual and collective strength

Opposition - Microsoft Internet Explorer

File   Edit   View   Favorites   Tools   Help

Address http://www.history.ohio-state.edu/projects/clash/NewWoman/opposition-page1.htm

Clash of Cultures in the 1910s and 1920s

Opposition

Introduction

Prohibition

Immigration Restriction & The Ku Klux Klan

The New Woman

   Image and Lifestyle

   Work, Education, and Reform

   Sexuality

   African American New Woman

   Opposition

Index

VULGAR PERSON - I'LL GO BACK TO THE HOTEL - THE SIGHTS HERE ARE DISGUSTING!

Many people in the 1910s and 1920s w alarmed by the new woman phenomenon. popular magazines throughout the peri writers called for a return to old-fashion morals and codes of behavior that had be discarded by much of the youn, generation. Men and women alike w critics of the new woman, and soc agencies joined parents in attempting return to Victorian standards of conduct, which women were supposed to be sexua passionless. Middle-class women to leadership roles through volunta organizations and social work, in some wa transgressing conventional gender roles in other ways reinforcing them. During First World War, the Young Women's Christian Association aided young urban women

Done   Internet

▲ The woman of the twenties was physically fit, flirtatious, competent, and confident. Past generations of women were not always able to show these qualities. For this, many looked down upon the youth of the day and felt their morals were lacking.

and consecrate all America, materially and spiritually, body and soul, to national defense.[1]

After demanding a reduction from wartime spending, Harding turned this phrase:

"Our most dangerous tendency is to expect too much of government, and at the same time do for it too little."[2] President John F. Kennedy would provide similar remarks in his inaugural address forty years later.

Harding concluded his speech by saying:

Tools   Search   Notes   Discuss   Go!

We ought to find a way to guard against the perils and penalties of unemployment. We want an America of homes, illumined with hope and happiness, where mothers, freed from the necessity of long hours of toil beyond their own doors, may preside as befits the hearthstone of American citizenship. We want the cradle of American childhood rocked under conditions so wholesome and so hopeful that no blight may touch it in its development.[3]

For the United States to go back to a normal way of life was easier said than done. There were the so-called "rebels" of society that danced in cabarets, drank bootleg gin, and made fun of "normal" Americans through plays and novels. The "normal" people, who did not like the rebels, tried to force their way of life on others by persecuting radicals, enforcing Prohibition, and fighting to ban the teaching of evolution in public schools.

Under the Harding administration, the country plunged into the Jazz Age with its mixed morals that created public support for Prohibition while bootleg whisky continued to flow freely, even in the White House.[4]

With such cultural change going on around him, Harding was bound to upset people no matter what he did. Still, by the end of the decade, Harding would be considered one of the worst presidents to ever serve the country. That is something that neither Harding, nor anyone that knew him from his days in Ohio, could have ever imagined.

Back	Forward	Stop	Review	Home	Explore	Favorites	History

Chapter 2 ▶

Younger Years, 1865–1891

Warren Gamaliel Harding was the first of eight children born to George and Phoebe Harding. He was born on November 2, 1865, on a farm near Corsica (today Blooming Grove), Ohio.

Warren G. Harding was a descendant of an English family that had originally landed in Plymouth, Massachusetts, in 1624.

▶ Growing Up

The Harding farm was located in Morrow County in north-central Ohio. Warren G. Harding's early years were filled with the day-to-day chores that were part of life on farms in those days.

When Warren was eight, his father became a homeopathic doctor. Homeopathic medicine is based on the theory of Dr. Samuel Hahnemann, which holds that a drug that would produce certain disease symptoms in a healthy person would cure a sick person exhibiting the same symptoms. Soon the young Harding was traveling with his father on horse-and-buggy calls to patients.

As a boy, Warren attended grammar schools at Corsica and Caledonia, both towns in Ohio. It was while he was attending school in Caledonia that Warren's father became part-owner of a weekly newspaper, the *Caledonia Argus.* Warren learned to set type for the newspaper. Soon young Harding's interests were fixed on newspaper work. Besides learning how to set type, he also ran the press and cleaned ink from the press rollers.

By the time he was fourteen, Warren was sent by his family to Ohio Central College in Iberia, Ohio. While attending college, Warren played the alto horn and edited the school yearbook. After just three years, Warren graduated from college.

At seventeen, he took a job as a teacher in a country school just outside of Marion, Ohio, for thirty dollars per month. He quit the teaching job after one term, feeling that he was not suited for it.

In the meantime, the Harding family moved to Marion in 1882. Warren's father, who did not seem to have much success in business, moved there hoping to improve the family's fortune.

After quitting his job as a teacher, Warren moved back to Marion with his family. He tried his hand at studying law and selling insurance but preferred shooting pool and playing poker with his friends. His greatest early success came in helping to organize the Citizen's Cornet Band of Marion, which won third place in a state band festival.[1]

Harding the Newspaperman

By the time he was nineteen, Harding was a reporter for the weekly *Marion Democratic Mirror*, earning one dollar a week. Unfortunately this job lasted only a few weeks. Harding happened to be a big supporter of James G. Blaine, the Republican presidential candidate in the 1884 national election. The owner of the paper happened to be a Democrat.

Being fired did not dampen Harding's love for newspapers. Shortly afterward, Harding gathered two friends, John Sickel and Jack Warwick, and between them they scraped together three hundred dollars and bought a daily newspaper, the *Marion Star*.

▲ Harding's love of newspaper work led him to buy the Marion Star, where he worked as the paper's editor and publisher.

The first edition of the revived newspaper came out on November 26, 1884. A weekly subscription to the paper cost ten cents. Even though his two partners eventually dropped out of the partnership, Harding continued to keep the paper in business.

Because the *Star* was considered politically independent, Harding started a separate *Weekly Star* that supported the Republican Party.

Battling with two other local papers for advertising dollars, the tobacco-chewing Harding joined in the rough-and-tumble "yellow" journalism of the times. These journalists and newspapers sometimes published material of questionable validity in order to sell papers.[2]

In 1891, at the age of twenty-five, Harding married Florence Mabel Kling DeWolfe, a thirty-year-old divorcée. She was the daughter of a well-known Marion banker, considered the richest man in the area.

Unfortunately, Flossie, as she was known as by her friends, had been deserted by her husband and disowned by her father. At the time of her marriage to Harding, she was struggling to support herself and her child by giving piano lessons.[3]

▲ *Florence Mabel Kling DeWolfe was strong-willed and self-reliant. After marrying Harding in 1891, "Flossie" helped her husband in his business and political endeavors.*

▲ *Turning the tables: On the White House lawn, Florence Harding operates a movie camera, perhaps capturing on film some of the White House photographers who were more often taking pictures of her and her husband.*

Florence eventually took over the business of running the *Marion Star* and helped Harding build it into a prosperous daily newspaper. Harding would eventually become director of several corporations and a trustee of the Trinity Baptist Church.

Florence's domineering manner led Harding to jokingly called her "Duchess."[4] However, the future president would soon appreciate her toughness as Flossie was to become the driving force behind Warren G. Harding's political success.

Entering Politics,
1892–1918

Warren Harding's first attempt at a political office ended in defeat. In 1892, at the age of twenty-seven, Harding ran in the race for county auditor but lost overwhelmingly.

Following the election, Harding commented wryly in the *Star* that the opposition Democrat won because he "had an easy mark for an opponent."[1]

Still, the defeat did not stop Harding from running for another political position. Thanks to his newspaper, the *Star*, which was becoming an influential voice in the Republican Party, Harding was becoming a very popular speaker on the political campaign circuit.

▶ State Senator Harding

By 1899, Harding had become an established figure in Ohio politics. That year at the Republican convention, Harding was nominated for the state senate. He won the election, and at thirty-four, became a state senator.

During this first term in the Ohio legislature, Harding showed what type of a loyal supporter he was to party leaders. He worked hard to become popular with his fellow lawmakers.

To show their thanks for the hard work Harding had done for the Republican Party, Republicans suspended a long-standing rule against renominating a state senator for reelection in his district.[2] Harding ran again and won a second term.

Lieutenant Governor

Warren Harding's star continued to rise in Ohio politics. By 1903, he was nominated for lieutenant governor, and once again, Harding was victorious in the election.

Surprisingly, at the end of his term as lieutenant governor, Harding went back to his newspaper career in Marion. At the time, some felt that he had gotten out of politics because he saw a Republican defeat coming in the next election. Others believed he was biding his time, waiting for a higher office to run for.

Harding Defeated in Run for Governor

By 1909, Harding had indeed decided to run for that higher office. That year he won the Republican nomination for governor of Ohio. His campaign was handled by Harry M. Daugherty. Daugherty was a lawyer who would later play an important role in Harding's presidential run.

Because of a split in the Republican Party that year, Harding was soundly defeated in the election by the incumbent governor, Judson Harmon, a Democrat.

Harry Daugherty (center) would go on to play an important role in Warren G. Harding's political career—not necessarily for the good, however.

Tools   Search   Notes   Discuss   Go!

▶ Harding Gains National Prominence

In 1912, Harding gained national recognition as a delegate to the Republican National Convention. He was selected to place President William Howard Taft's name in nomination for Taft's second term. It was said that this honor gave Harding a greater thrill than his own nomination as president years later.

Harding impressed many on hand with his public-speaking ability, although his speech for Taft was delivered among jeers and catcalls from Theodore Roosevelt's supporters. Nevertheless, Taft was easily nominated the Republican Party's presidential candidate, and Roosevelt became a third-party candidate for the Bull Moose or Progressive Party. In the election, the split in the Republican vote helped Woodrow Wilson, a Democrat, to be elected president.

Four years later, Warren G. Harding would return to the national spotlight at the Republican National Convention. As the party's chairman, he would deliver the keynote address, this time to a less hostile crowd.

Harding served as an Ohio senator to ▶ the U.S. Congress from 1915 to 1921.

▶ United States Senate Awaits Harding

By 1914, Daugherty and Flossie had convinced Harding to run for the United States Senate. Despite the fact that Ohio's largest newspaper, the *Cleveland Plain Dealer*, labeled Harding as a "spokesman of the past," Harding soundly defeated Timothy Hogan, the Democratic candidate.

Harding seemed to really enjoy his first term as U.S. senator. As he had done in the state senate, Harding worked hard to become popular with his fellow senators.

If there was a negative side to Harding, it was his unimpressive record as a lawmaker. When it came time to answer roll calls, Harding failed to respond almost half the time. Many felt at the time that Harding spent a great deal of his efforts as a senator trying to find jobs for his friends instead of studying legislation and voting on it.

When he did introduce measures to be voted on, most were of no real significance. When he did have something of importance to present, Harding showed little conviction in its presentation.

Harding usually voted his party line: Republican. The Ohio senator opposed the League of Nations and favored high tariffs. He did, however, vote for women's suffrage.

Chapter 4 ▶

An Unlikely Candidate, 1919–1920

By 1919, rumors were beginning to spread throughout the United States that Harding could be considered a possible presidential candidate. There were even some newspapers that were mentioning Harding as a compromise candidate, if none of the other candidates had enough support. In these cases a deal is struck to find a candidate that everyone can agree on.

Harry Daugherty was persistent in urging Harding to run for president. Because he liked the life of a senator and because he recognized his own limitations, Harding did not want to run.[1] He truly believed that he could not win the nomination or election. He refused to make up his mind to announce his candidacy. Finally, Daugherty, assisted by Mrs. Harding, told Harding that by not announcing his candidacy for president, he could jeopardize his chances of being elected for a second term to the U.S. Senate.

In December 1919, Harding finally wrote a letter to the Republican committee in Ohio, announcing his intentions of running for president.

Daugherty decided to have Harding enter three state primaries where he figured to do well: Ohio, Indiana, and Montana. Harding won in Ohio, but lost badly in Indiana and Montana. Once again, Harding believed that he was not a strong-enough candidate for president. However, Daugherty, along with Florence Harding, urged Harding to continue to run.

Calvin Coolidge (right) was chosen as Harding's running mate for the campaign of 1920.

The Smoke-Filled Room

When the Republican National Convention opened in Chicago in June 1920, Harding was considered a long shot at winning the nomination. The favorites among the delegates were Governor Frank O. Lowden of Illinois and Major General Leonard Wood, former army chief of staff.

On the first day of voting, the convention adjourned until morning in a deadlock after just four ballots. That night a group of powerful Republican political bosses and senators met at the Blackstone Hotel in downtown Chicago. In a room that Daugherty referred to as "smoke-filled," these power brokers met into the night to elect a candidate for president.

These influential Republicans decided that they did not want Wood or Lowden. After discussing all of the possibilities, the group passed their support to Harding.

There was some suspicion of Harding's private life. He was called to the hotel and asked bluntly if he had anything in his life or background that might embarrass the party. Harding was left alone to consider the question, and after a few minutes of thought, Harding told the group that his past was an open record. In turn, the group assured Harding of the nomination.[2] What Harding did not feel compelled to reveal in public were his extramarital affairs with two women. One of those women had given birth to Harding's illegitimate child, a daughter, just a year earlier.

The next day, even though Wood and Lowden continued to hold first and second place through eight ballots, Harding's vote total was slowly beginning to increase. Finally, on the ninth ballot, Harding moved into the lead.

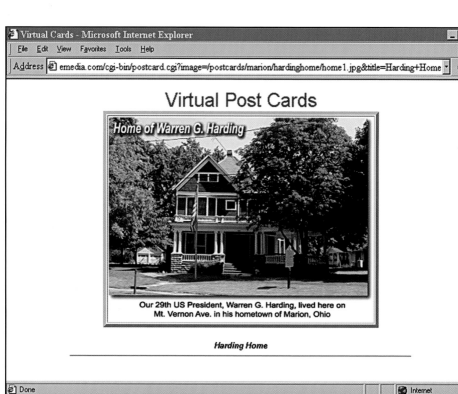

Virtual Post Cards

Home of Warren G. Harding

Our 29th US President, Warren G. Harding, lived here on Mt. Vernon Ave. in his hometown of Marion, Ohio

Harding Home

Harding campaigned for the presidential election of 1920 from the front porch of his home in Marion, Ohio.

On the tenth ballot, Harding won the nomination with 692.5 of the convention's 984 votes. Harding's comment, as quoted by the *Literary Digest,* was typical: "I feel like a man who goes in on a pair of eights and comes out with aces full."[3]

Governor Calvin Coolidge of Massachusetts was nominated as Harding's running mate.

The Democrats nominated James M. Cox, governor of Ohio, as their presidential candidate and Franklin D. Roosevelt, assistant secretary of the navy under President Wilson, as vice president.

The Front-Porch Candidate

Harding was well aware that to win the presidential election, he would have to campaign nationally. Instead, he decided to do a lot of his campaigning from his home in Marion, Ohio. His campaign became known as a "front porch" campaign.

He met thousands of people, including visiting delegations from other states, on his porch. In the fall, Harding did some campaigning aboard a train that made a series of stops across the United States.

In the November 2, 1920, presidential election, Harding easily defeated Cox. American voters were tired of the government restrictions and hardships that had been imposed on them by World War I. They wanted a complete change in administration. Voters wanted back the days when America would not have to look beyond its own borders.

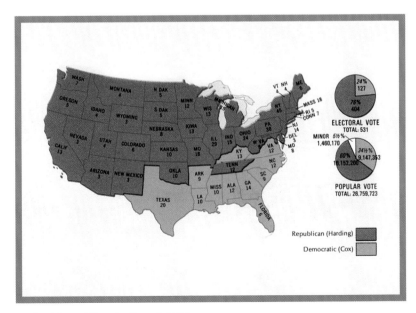

▲ Map of the election of 1920.

Harding received 16,143,407 popular votes compared to Cox's 9,130,328 votes. In the electoral college the Republican candidate won 404 votes to 127.

With his victory, Warren G. Harding became the first man elected to the presidency while serving in the U.S. Senate. The election of 1920 was also notable for some others firsts. It was the first presidential election in which all women could vote, since the Nineteenth Amendment was ratified in August of that year. It was also the first election whose results were broadcast over the radio. Although there were not that many radio stations even on the air at the time, station KDKA in Pittsburgh could be heard over most of the eastern half of the United States, as election results were read from a telegraph ticker.

One of the more interesting stories of the 1920 election involved Eugene V. Debs, the third-party candidate. Debs, the Socialist Party's nominee, came in third in the race, but he received nearly one million votes. And he accomplished that while he was in prison. He had been arrested in 1918, during World War I, for making a speech against the war. Debs, who conducted his entire 1920 campaign from prison, had been sentenced to ten years, but President Harding had Debs released from prison on Christmas Day of 1921, commuting his sentence to time served.

President Harding, 1921–1923

One of the first things that Warren Harding did following his election was to begin choosing his cabinet. If there was one thing that Harding would do during his administration it would be to depend on his cabinet and Congress to provide leadership.

It would be his faith in some members of his cabinet that would eventually lead to his demise as president. Some of his cabinet appointments were close political friends. Others represented various powerful interests in the Republican Party.

▲ Part of Harding's downfall was his reliance on his cabinet. This photograph captures Harding with his cabinet shortly after his inauguration.

▲ Secretary of the Navy Edwin Denby became embroiled in the Teapot Dome scandal by allowing oil reserves that had belonged to the navy to be handed over to the Interior Department. Here, he is surrounded by reporters during the Teapot Dome investigation.

Three appointments in particular would eventually prove to be his undoing. They were Secretary of the Interior Albert B. Fall, an ex-senatorial colleague and friend of western oilmen who had contributed big money to the Harding presidential campaign fund; Secretary of the Navy Edwin Denby, a lawyer who had made a lot of money in the automobile business and had served as a congressman from Michigan; and Attorney General Harry Daugherty, the mastermind behind Harding's move to the White House.

▶ The Ohio Gang

While Harding may have had a formal cabinet, a great deal of the real business conducted by the Harding administration took place at night at the White House. That is when Harding hosted poker and drinking parties. They were regularly attended by Jesse Smith, a Harding friend of questionable reputation, Fall, and Daugherty, as well as other cronies and hangers-on.

Friends and acquaintances of Harding and Daugherty from Ohio started heading to Washington, D.C., for jobs. Headquarters of the "Ohio Gang," as they were called, was the "Little Green House" at 1625 K Street. Government favors and appointments were bought and sold at this address. There has never been any evidence to show that Harding actually sanctioned what was going on. His friends just basically knew that Harding would agree with their suggestions in order to please them.[1]

Harding on the International Scene

Harding was quick to earn the respect of other world leaders. One of the first things he did was to call the Washington Conference for the Limitation of Armament

▲ Attending a baseball game in 1922 are, left to right, Secretary of Commerce Herbert Hoover, Florence Harding, President Harding, Lou Hoover (Mrs. Herbert Hoover), and Attorney General Harry Daugherty.

in 1921. The United States used this conference to push for the end of the arms race between nations. The country also asked for the actual destruction of existing war machines.

Because the Republican-controlled Senate had failed to ratify the Versailles Treaty during Wilson's term, the United States had not yet formally ended World War I. The treaty was not ratified because a majority in Congress were opposed to its provision that would make the United States a member of the League of Nations. It was thus up to Harding's administration to make a formal peace with Germany. In 1921, Congress passed a joint resolution that ended "the state of war between the Imperial German government and the United States of America." The resolution's signing, however, was not exactly handled in public or with great fanfare.

On July 2, 1921, Harding had been playing golf when a White House aide arrived with the joint resolution. Harding left the golf course and went to the home of Senator Joseph Frelinghuysen of New Jersey, whom he had been visiting. Harding is said to have then signed the treaty that ended World War I while Frelinghuysen's dog "sniffed his shoes."[2] The president then hurried back to his golf game.

▶ Harding on the National Scene

One of Harding's strong points was his ability to prepare a national budget. The person who helped him put together that budget was Charles G. Dawes of Chicago, first director of the budget, considered one of the best appointments to the Harding administration.

Harding also worked very hard at having the steel industry lower the twelve-hour workday. That was the

Former President Woodrow Wilson gave birth to the idea of the League of Nations, but the United States never became a member of the international organization.

standard of the industry at the time. Although Harding never lived to see it, steel companies eventually lowered the hours in a workday.

With Harding's approval, Congress increased protective tariffs to new highs with the Fordney-McCumber Act of 1922. The president, though, vetoed a big soldier's bonus bill for the veterans of World War I. Harding pointed out that the bill would not provide the necessary additional revenues to pay the bonus.

Government Scandals

Corruption was in the air at the start of the 1920s. The United States government was active in the disposal of alien property worth millions of dollars, in the sale of surplus merchant ships, and in the management of rich oil lands. Opportunities for gaining wealth illegally by using one's position in government happened quite a bit during the "Roaring Twenties."

When the elections of 1922 took place, the Republican majority was reduced in both houses of Congress.

Harding was worried that the election proved that the country had lost faith in his administration.

Late in 1922, Harding found out about problems in the Veterans Bureau. Illegal operations were taking place. Harding was quite upset when he found out that the head of the Veterans Bureau, Charles R. Forbes, one of his close friends, was deeply involved. Forbes was soon replaced.

In March 1923, Harding got another shock when Charles F. Cramer, the attorney for the Veterans Bureau, committed suicide. Cramer had been an aide to Forbes.

△ After resigning as director of the Veterans Bureau on February 15, 1923, Charles R. Forbes was convicted of fraud, conspiracy, and bribery, and received a two-year sentence.

After news of the Harding administration's many scandals spread, the president decided to take a train trip across the country in an attempt to regain confidence in his administration.

Harding received yet another shock in May when Jesse Smith, an assistant to Attorney General Daugherty, also took his own life. Smith had been ordered to leave Washington when the president found out about other scandals that were about to break. Before killing himself, Smith had destroyed all of his papers in an attempt to cover up any misdeeds.

Harding was a very worried man when he scheduled himself to go on a "voyage of understanding" beginning on June 20, 1923.

The train trip was to take the president across the North American continent and to Alaska in an attempt to gain support for his policies. It was to be a voyage that would take a great toll on Harding.

Chapter 6

A Tragic Ending, 1923

President Warren Harding set out from Washington on the "voyage of understanding" on June 20, 1923. He was a very worried man, disturbed over the tragic events that had taken the lives of two of his friends just weeks earlier.

When Harding got to Kansas City, he was paid a visit by Mrs. Albert Fall. Her husband had resigned as secretary of the interior a few months earlier. She told him of Falls' dealings and how her husband had accepted a bribe for leasing government-owned oil reserves to private companies.

By the time Harding reached Alaska in July, the president received a long message in code that had been sent to him from Washington. It brought troublesome news about

▲ Warren Harding takes a horseback ride through Zion National Park in Utah during his "voyage of understanding" tour.

▲ *Chief Justice William Howard Taft, left, and President Warren G. Harding, center, were two of the speakers at the dedication of the Lincoln Memorial, May 30, 1922. Abraham Lincoln's son Robert Todd Lincoln is to their right.*

a Senate investigation of oil leases. Harding began to repeatedly mutter comments about friends who had betrayed him.

Harding fell ill on July 27 while in Seattle. It was first diagnosed as indigestion. Later theories indicated that Harding may have suffered a heart attack.

All future appearances by the president were cancelled, although Harding's health seemed to be improving. On July 29, Harding arrived in San Francisco and seemed to be on the road to recovery.

Then what doctors diagnosed as pneumonia hit the president. Once again, Harding seemed to be recovering. Then at 7:35 P.M. on August 2, Warren Harding died.

The doctors, believing that a blood clot had traveled to the president's brain, asked for permission to perform an autopsy. Mrs. Harding refused. As a result, the exact cause of Harding's death remains in doubt to this day. Later, there was some speculation that the president might have been poisoned to prevent him from testifying against friends or to avoid the embarrassment of having to take the witness stand.[1] Without an autopsy, however, that theory cannot be verified.

▶ The Scandals Are Unearthed

The news of the scandals and the problems of Harding's administration had not yet become public at the time of his death. So, as Harding's body traveled in the funeral train across the United States on its return to Washington, thousands of mourners gathered along the tracks to pay their respects.

On August 8, services were held for Harding in Washington, D.C. From there Harding's body was taken back to his hometown of Marion, Ohio, for burial.

By the time Harding was buried, information regarding the "Teapot Dome scandal" was beginning to spread to the public.

Even before Harding's death, Senator Thomas J.

Upon the death of Warren G. Harding, Calvin Coolidge became the thirtieth president of the United States.

▲ *Lines of people wait to enter the United States Capitol Rotunda to pay their respects to the fallen president.*

Walsh of Montana had been growing suspicious of Secretary Fall's business dealings. Fall had opened up to private companies two huge oil fields that had been reserved for future naval needs.[2]

Control of the fields, Elk Hills in California and Teapot Dome in Wyoming, had been transferred from the Navy Department to the Department of the Interior in 1921 with Harding's approval. Suspicions of bribery were heightened by the fact that Fall had made lavish improvements on his New Mexico ranch with no sufficient visible source of income.[3]

After further investigation by Walsh, it was discovered that Fall had taken bribes worth more than $400,000. Following years of hearings and court cases, Fall was convicted of bribery and sent to prison in 1929.

▲ *A crowd gathers for Warren G. Harding's burial at Marion Cemetery, in Ohio. An elaborate memorial would later be built for Harding and his wife.*

Two more of Harding's friends, former Director of the Veterans Bureau Charles R. Forbes and John W. Thompson, an official of one of the firms that Forbes had been doing business with, were brought to trial and convicted. Both were sentenced to prison terms.

Even Harding's old friend, Attorney General Harry Daugherty, was brought to trial in 1924 on charges of conspiracy. Following two trials which ended in a hung jury, the case was dropped.

▷ Little Evidence

How much President Harding knew about the corruption among his friends and associates will never be known. Following his death, Mrs. Harding burned most of his papers and correspondence with the individuals involved in the scandals. She even recovered and destroyed all personal letters that Harding had written to others.

Florence Harding died a little over a year after the president, on November 21, 1924. As a result, historians

do not have too much to work with in their search for facts regarding Harding and his dealings with his associates.

In 1931, at the dedication of the Harding tomb in Marion, President Herbert Hoover, who had been secretary of commerce in Harding's cabinet, said, "Here was a man whose soul was seared by a great disillusionment. We saw him gradually weaken, not only from physical exhaustion, but also from mental anxiety . . . Warren Harding had a dim realization that he had been betrayed by a few of the men whom he had believed were his devoted friends. That was the tragedy of the life of Warren Harding."[4]

▶ Harding's Legacy

Most historians rank Harding as one of the weakest presidents. In a 2000 poll conducted by the *Wall Street Journal* and the Federalist Society, he ranked thirty-eighth out of the thirty-nine presidents they assessed. Yet some of the same historians that criticize him recognize that the very qualities that made him weak also made him appealing in 1920.

Harding simply failed because he was weak-willed and was a poor judge of character. The people he thought

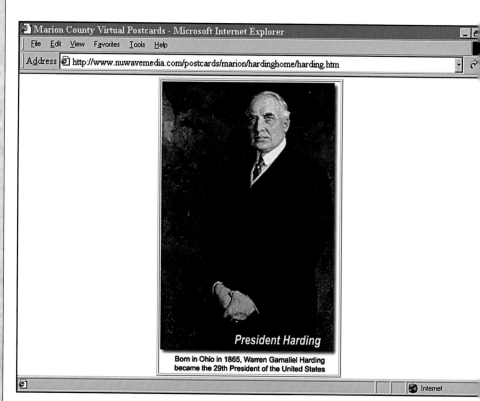

President Harding

Born in Ohio in 1865, Warren Gamaliel Harding became the 29th President of the United States

▲ Historians often rank Warren G. Harding as one of the United States' least effective presidents.

were his friends were the same people that eventually got into trouble and possibly led to the health problems that cost Harding his life.

Even at the one hundredth anniversary of Harding's birth, the celebration that took place in Mario, Ohio, turned out to be dismal.

But not all historians are as critical of Warren G. Harding. Historian Francis Russell wrote in the foreword of his book on the twenty-ninth president: "Harding, with his tarnished reputation, has never claimed the serious attention of historians. In this he has been the most neglected of presidents."[5]

Chapter Notes

Chapter 1. Inauguration, 1921

1. Warren G. Harding, as posted on the Internet, "Inaugural Address: Friday, March 4, 1921," 2003, *Bartleby.com*, <http://www.bartleby.com/124/pres46.html> (March 10, 2003).

2. Ibid.

3. Ibid.

4. David C. Whitney, *The American Presidents* (Garden City, N.Y.: Doubleday & Company, 1985), p. 240.

Chapter 2. Younger Years, 1865–1891

1. David C. Whitney, *The American Presidents* (Garden City, N.Y.: Doubleday & Company, 1985), p. 240.

2. Ibid., p. 241.

3. William A. DeGregorio, *The Complete Book of U.S. Presidents* (New York: Wings Books, 1997), p. 434.

4. Whitney, p. 241.

Chapter 3. Entering Politics, 1892–1918

1. David C. Whitney, *The American Presidents* (Garden City, N.Y.: Doubleday & Company, 1985), p. 241.

2. Ibid., pp. 241–242.

Chapter 4. An Unlikely Candidate, 1919–1920

1. David C. Whitney, *The American Presidents* (Garden City, N.Y.: Doubleday & Company, 1985) p. 243.

2. William A. DeGregorio, *The Complete Book of U.S. Presidents* (New York: Wings Books, 1997), p. 437.

3. Paul Sann, as reposted by the Estate of Paul Sann, "Gee, What a President He'd Make," n.d., *The Lawless Decade,* <http://www.paulsann.org/thelawlessdecade/new1921.html> (March 10, 2003).

Chapter 5. President Harding, 1921–1923

1. David C. Whitney, *The American Presidents* (Garden City, N.Y.: Doubleday & Company, 1985) pp. 245–246.

2. William A. DeGregorio, *The Complete Book of U.S. Presidents* (New York: Wings Books, 1997), p. 440.

Chapter 6. A Tragic Ending, 1923

1. Philip B. Kunhardt, Jr., Philip B. Kunhardt III, and Peter W. Kunhardt, "The Return to Normalcy President," 2000, *The American President,* <http://www.americanpresident.org/KoTrain/Courses/WH/WH_In_Brief.htm> (March 10, 2003).

2. David C. Whitney, *The American Presidents* (Garden City, N.Y.: Doubleday & Company, 1985), p. 248.

3. Ibid.

4. Ibid, p. 249.

5. Francis Russell, *The Shadow of Blooming Grove* (New York: McGraw-Hill Book Company, 1968), foreword.

Further Reading

Anthony, Carl Sferrazza. *Florence Harding: The First Lady, the Jazz Age & the Death of America's Most Scandalous President.* New York: Morrow/Avon, 1998.

Canadeo, Anne and Richard G. Young, eds. *Warren G. Harding: Twenty-Ninth President of the United States.* Ada, Okla.: Garrett Educational Corporation, 1990.

Clare, John D., ed. *The First World War.* New York: Harcourt Children's Books, 1995.

Dudley, William, ed. *World War I.* Farmington Hills, Mich.: Gale Group, 1997.

Hargrove, Jim. *The Story of the Teapot Dome Scandal.* Danbury, Conn.: Children's Press, 1989.

Keene, Jennifer D. *The United States & the First World War.* Boston: Addison-Wesley Longman, Inc., 2000.

Romero, Francine Sanders. *Presidents from Theodore Roosevelt Through Coolidge. 1901–1929: Debating the Issues in Pro & Con Primary Documents.* Westport, Conn.: Greenwood Publishing Group, Inc., 2000.

Stalcup, Brenda. *Women's Suffrage.* Farmington Hills, Mich.: Gale Group, 2000.

Weber, Michael. *Taft, Wilson, Harding, and Coolidge.* Vero Beach, Fla.: Rourke Corporation, 1996.